I0817577

The True Ugly Duckling

How Hans Christian Andersen Became a Swan

Written by Sandra Nickel Illustrated by Calvin Nicholls

LEVINE QUERIDO

SKOLE

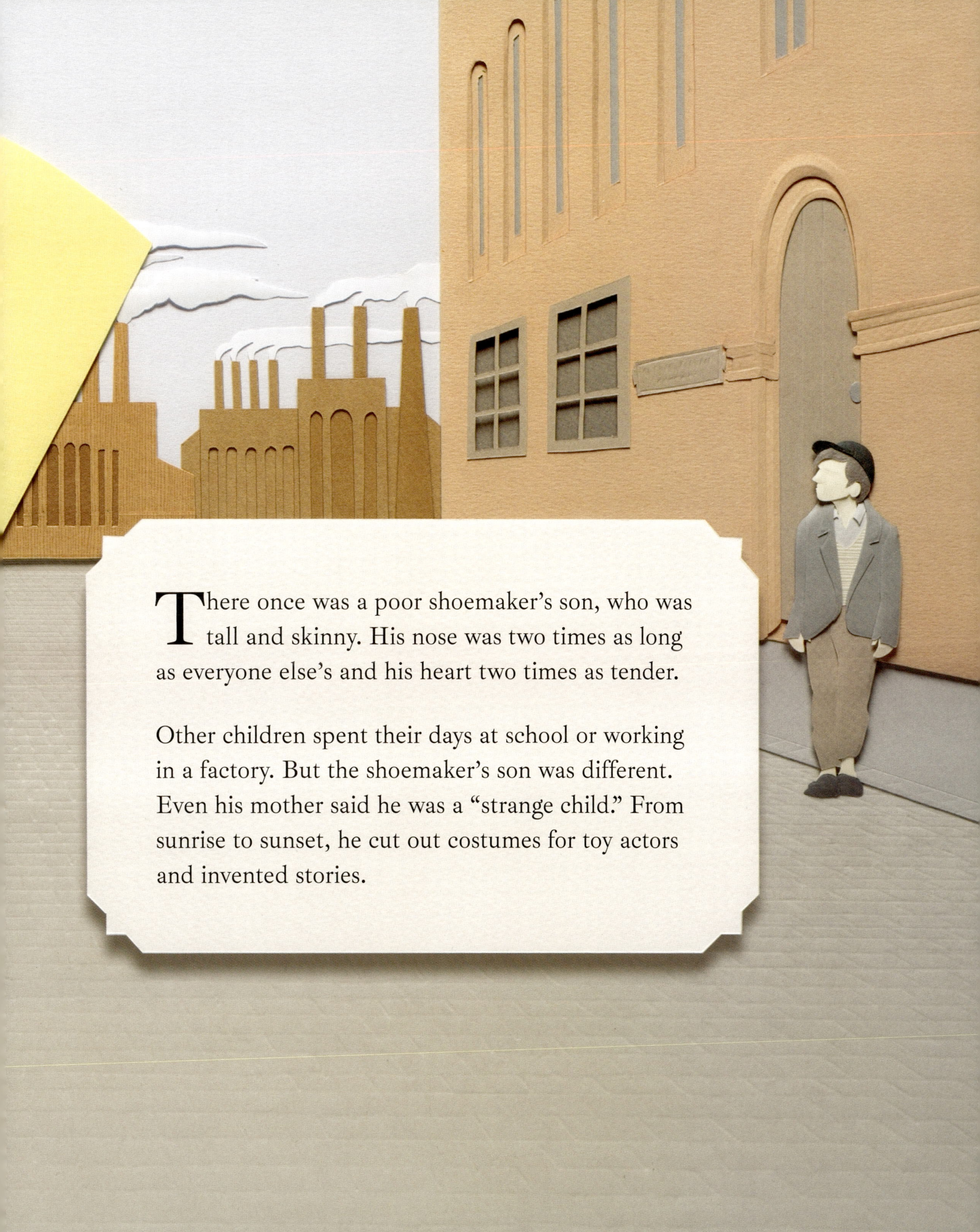

There once was a poor shoemaker's son, who was tall and skinny. His nose was two times as long as everyone else's and his heart two times as tender.

Other children spent their days at school or working in a factory. But the shoemaker's son was different. Even his mother said he was a "strange child." From sunrise to sunset, he cut out costumes for toy actors and invented stories.

When the boy's stories were ready, he performed for whomever he could find. Workers in the factory. Children on the street. Neighbors in their homes.

He did whatever he could to make the townsfolk like his stories. He jumped like an acrobat and made faces like a mime.

A few kind neighbors gave him coins. But the children chased him. And the workers held him down, hooting, until the boy cried and squirmed away.

Back home, the boy soothed his wounded heart by cutting out shapes from cloth.

He knew there must be more in the big world than his little village. So, he took his few coins and scissors, left his mother behind, and went to the greatest city in the world: Copenhagen. The city of the King.

He first went to the Royal Theater. After all, he had been performing his whole life!

But he spoke like a country duck and, for that matter, acted like one too. The manager took one look and listen and booted him out of the theater.

The boy went to the dance school at the Court Theater, sure that he would dance as well as the King's noble dancers.

But his long left foot got tangled in his long right foot, and he looked nothing like the other students gliding across the room like swans.

The boy next went to the Royal Theater's Boys' Choir, certain his voice would rise in the air like a nightingale's, high, high, high to the palace itself.

And it did.

But only for a little while, until his voice changed, and it became less like a nightingale's and more like a toad's. The director sent him away and told him to never come back.

The boy's few coins were long gone. What was he to do alone in that big, big world?

The boy had one last idea. He invented a play and sent it off to the directors of the Royal Theater.

One director said it would never, ever—even if it was the last play in the world—be performed. The other director said there were a few jewels in what the boy had written. He arranged for school and sent the boy off to start at the very beginning.

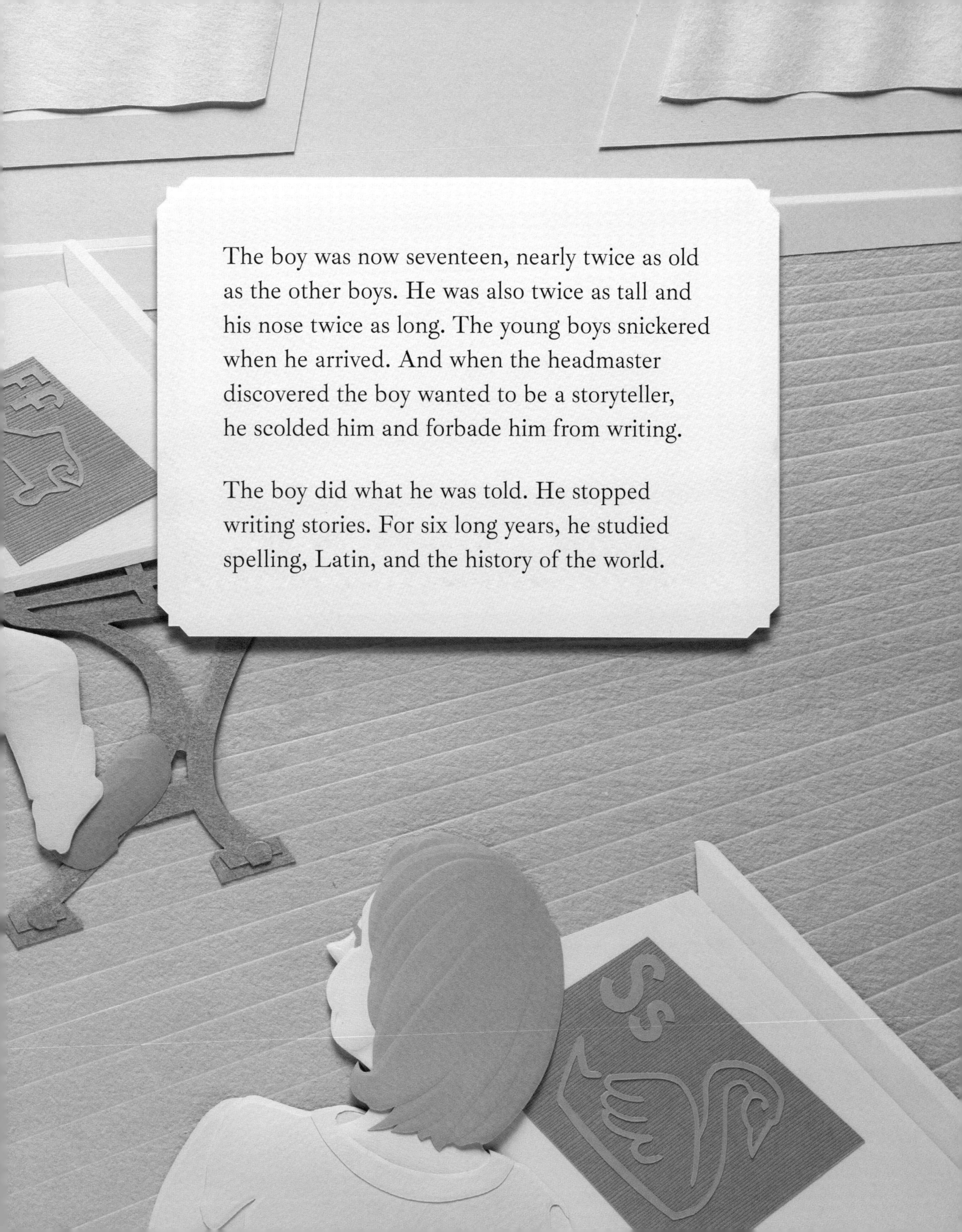

The boy was now seventeen, nearly twice as old as the other boys. He was also twice as tall and his nose twice as long. The young boys snickered when he arrived. And when the headmaster discovered the boy wanted to be a storyteller, he scolded him and forbade him from writing.

The boy did what he was told. He stopped writing stories. For six long years, he studied spelling, Latin, and the history of the world.

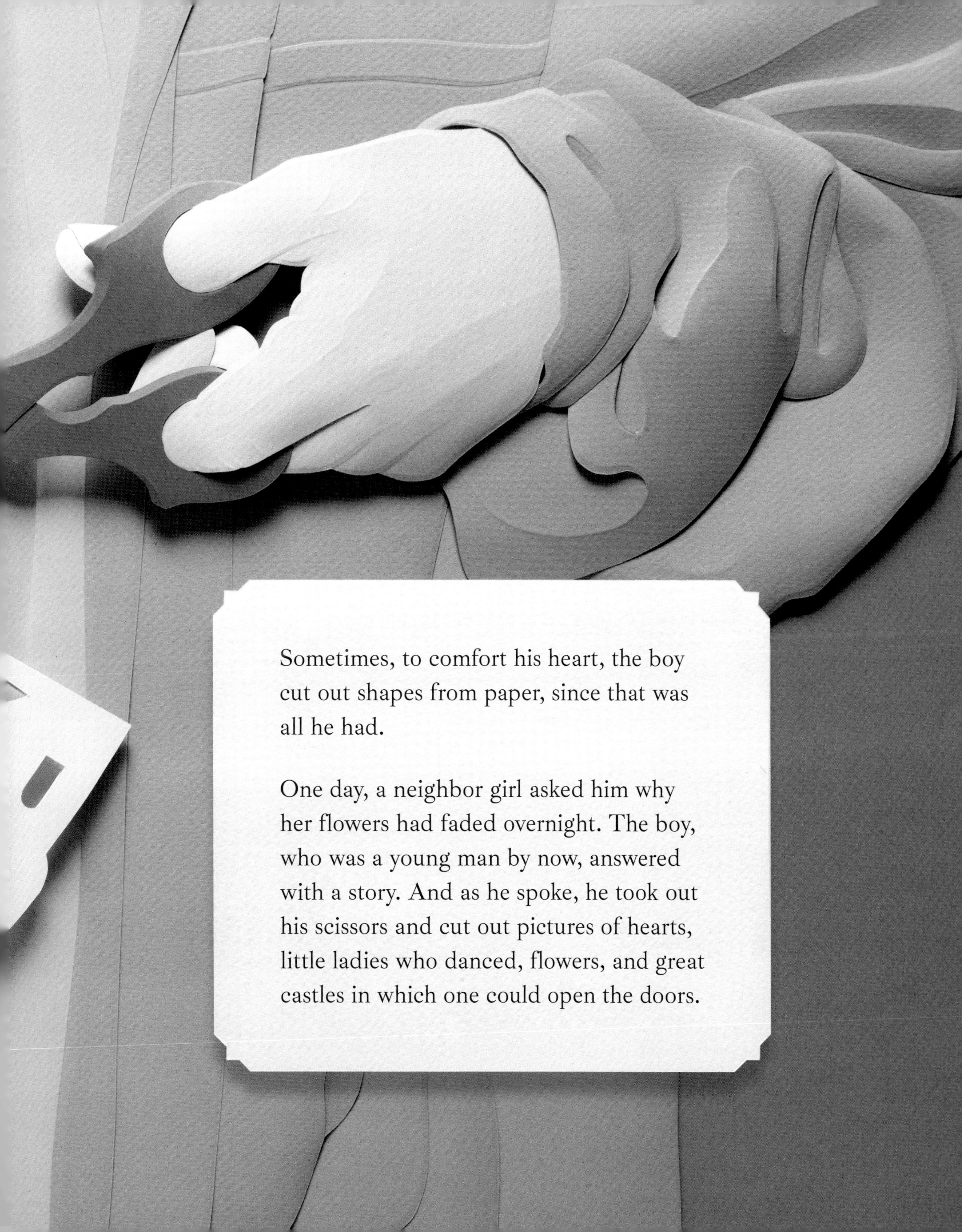

Sometimes, to comfort his heart, the boy cut out shapes from paper, since that was all he had.

One day, a neighbor girl asked him why her flowers had faded overnight. The boy, who was a young man by now, answered with a story. And as he spoke, he took out his scissors and cut out pictures of hearts, little ladies who danced, flowers, and great castles in which one could open the doors.

The girl loved the story so much that the shoemaker's son took a pen and wrote it down. He then persuaded a maker of books to print it, along with three tales that had long been known, but that he now told in his own, original way.

The adults of Copenhagen thought his stories were strange.

But, the children! The children of Copenhagen adored every word.

Now that he had started, the shoemaker's son couldn't stop. Whenever he met children, he told stories. The more he told, the more he wrote. And the more he wrote, the more children read.

Before long, even adults were reading about a one-legged tin soldier who yearned for love. A poor match girl. A mermaid who gave up her voice for a prince.

Suddenly, it seemed as if everyone wanted to meet the shoemaker's son. Even the King in Copenhagen and countesses and queens invited him to their castles.

The shoemaker's son often felt like a country duck with all these noble people. But after dinner, everyone crowded around. As he took his scissors from his pocket, they hushed their voices. And as he weaved magic with his words and scissors, he felt like the most beautiful swan of all.

AUTHOR'S NOTE

Experts believe that Hans Christian Andersen was likely on the autism spectrum. He may have also had Marfan syndrome, which may result in unusually long noses, arms, and legs. Around the time I discovered this, I learned that Andersen said *The Ugly Duckling*—a story of social exclusion and hope—mirrored his own life.

Curious about his childhood, I read biographies written by others and by Andersen himself. His growing-up years seemed familiar to me—his differentness, his hyperfocus, the solace he found in stories. I have three generations of neurodivergent women in my family, and we have each grappled with our places in the world.

Believing that fairy tales reflect aspects of our inner world, I took up my pen and wrote this biography in the form of Andersen's fairy tales. I hoped that by following the arc of *The Ugly Duckling*, readers might be able to relate more easily to the life of a "strange child," who yearned to be accepted. Most importantly, I wanted to show that Andersen used his originality—even the reassuring, repetitive movement of cutting out shapes—to find his own place in the world.

By drawing on his experiences and innate differences, Andersen wrote about characters who were traditionally underrepresented or oppressed—children, the poor, and those who did not conform to social expectations. By doing so, Andersen's stories resonated with readers and entered the worldwide consciousness. His fairy tales are now read in 160 languages and have inspired ballets, plays, operas, films—and children's imaginations everywhere.

SELECT BIBLIOGRAPHY

- Andersen, Hans Christian. *The Fairy Tale of My Life*. New York: First Cooper Square, 2000. Originally published in English, London 1871.
- Andersen, Hans Christian. *Tales: Little Ida's Flowers*. Bartleby.com. Originally published 1909–1914 by Harvard Classics.
- Andersen, Hans Christian. *The Ugly Duckling*. Bartleby.com. Originally published 1909–1914 by Harvard Classics.
- Bredsdorff, Elias, *Hans Christian Andersen: The Story of His Life and Work 1805–75*. New York: Phaidon, 1975.
- Brust, Beth Wagner. *The Amazing Paper Cuttings of Hans Christian Andersen*. Boston: Houghton Mifflin, 1994.
- "Hans Christian Andersen and the Art of Cut Paper," Meridian International Center, http://www.meridian.org/wildswans/cutpaper.html.
- Wullschläger, Jackie. *Hans Christian Andersen: The Life of a Storyteller*. New York: Penguin, 2000.

CITATIONS

- "strange child": Andersen, *The Fairy Tale of My Life*, page 10.
- The phrase "hearts, little ladies who danced, flowers, and great castles in which one could open the doors" closely parallels Andersen's own words, "hearts, with little ladies in them who danced; flowers, and great castles in which one could open the doors": Andersen, *Tales: Little Ida's Flowers*.

To Eleanor and to all the others who have struggled on their ways to becoming a swan.
—S.N.

For my wife and three artist children, who know the reward of acting on inspiration.
—C.N.

This is an Arthur A. Levine book
Published by Levine Querido

LQ
LEVINE QUERIDO

Levine Querido
www.levinequerido.com • info@levinequerido.com

Levine Querido is distributed by Chronicle Books, LLC

Library of Congress Control Number: 2024950978

ISBN 978-1-64614-576-8

Printed and bound in China

Published February 2026
First Printing

Book design by David Caplan and Prashansa Thapa
The text type was set in Ibarra Real Nova.

The art for this book consists of low-relief sculptures, created using a variety of cover- and text-weight colored papers, with form and texture added through the use of embossing and cutting tools. Each sculpture was developed from sketch through patterns, assembled at an art table, and then captured by the artist using high-resolution photography under studio lighting.